19.50

$1-12-11$

CAMERA OPERATOR

By Geoffrey M. Horn

Reading Consultant: Susan Nations, M.Ed.,
author/literacy coach/consultant in literacy development

Gareth Stevens
Publishing

Please visit our web site at **www.garethstevens.com.**
For a free catalog describing Gareth Stevens Publishing's list of high-quality books,
call 1-800-542-2595 (USA) or 1-800-387-3178 (Canada).
Gareth Stevens Publishing's fax: 1-877-542-2596

Library of Congress Cataloging-in-Publication Data available on request from publisher.

ISBN-10: 1-4339-0001-7	ISBN-13: 978-1-4339-0001-3 (lib.bdg.)
ISBN-10: 1-4339-0165-X	ISBN-13: 978-1-4339-0165-2 (softcover)

This edition first published in 2009 by
Gareth Stevens Publishing
A Weekly Reader® Company
1 Reader's Digest Rd.
Pleasantville, NY 10570-7000 USA

Copyright © 2009 by Gareth Stevens, Inc.

Executive Managing Editor: Lisa M. Herrington
Creative Director: Lisa Donovan
Senior Editor: Barbara Bakowski
Editor: Joann Jovinelly
Designer: Paula Jo Smith
Photo Researcher: Kimberly Babbitt
Publisher: Keith Garton

Picture credits: Cover and title page: Kevin Fleming/Corbis; p. 4 Courtesy of Zeitgeist
Films, Ltd.; p. 5 Newscom; p. 6 Richard Smith/Corbis; p. 8 Todd France/Corbis; p. 10
Alamy; p. 12 Shutterstock; p. 13 Richard Heathcote/Getty Images; p. 14 Scott Boehm/Getty
Images; p. 15 Courtesy of Alan and Sarah Scott Gleiner; p. 17 Alamy; p. 18 Getty Images for
Pepsi; p. 21 Scott Gries/Getty Images; p. 22 Charley Gallay/Getty Images; p. 23 Christof
Koepsel/Bongarts/Getty Images; p. 25 Alamy; p. 27 Randy Belice/NBAE via Getty Images;
p. 28 Andy Lopusnak/Arena Football League via Getty Images

Printed in the United States of America

1 2 3 4 5 6 7 8 9 10 09 08

CONTENTS

Words in the glossary appear in **bold** type the first time they are used in the text.

CHAPTER 1
GETTING THE PICTURE

In 2005, Hurricane Katrina stormed toward the Gulf Coast. New Orleans couple Scott and Kimberly Roberts videotaped the Louisiana city. They recorded the people who left. They captured the stories of those who stayed behind. They witnessed amazing rescues and tragic losses. More important, they recorded people helping each other through a terrible crisis. Their efforts became a **documentary**.

Hurricane Katrina is the subject of the award-winning documentary *Trouble the Water*.

In 2008, the couple was honored at the famous Sundance Film Festival in Utah. Their documentary, *Trouble the Water*, received a prize. Suddenly, two people who had never before used a video camera were in the spotlight.

Camera operators are often on the go in poor weather conditions. This camera operator shoots in New Orleans, Louisiana, during Hurricane Katrina.

Video on the Go

To tell an exciting story, camera operators need to be where the action is. To get to that action, professional camera operators travel all over the world.

Do you want to see how gorillas live in Africa? Are you curious about Florida's alligators? Are you interested in learning about polar bears in the Arctic? Camera operators brave jungles, swamps, and even icebergs to shoot those videos.

Camera operators sometimes shoot outdoors for TV programs and travel videos. This cameraman's camouflage clothing helps him capture close-ups of wildlife.

Of course, not all camera operators travel to exotic places or extreme settings. Many work on film sets and in TV studios in big cities. Some camera operators work on the go with local reporters.

Camera Operators and Editors

In the United States, about 27,000 people work as camera operators. They shoot video and film in different ways. For example, TV camera operators shoot video that is shown live from local studios. Video camera operators record video on tape. (Newer cameras often use memory cards or disk drives.) Motion picture camera operators shoot film for big-budget movies.

Another 21,000 people in the United States work as film or video editors. They take **raw footage** from the camera and turn it into a finished product. Some camera operators do their own editing.

Getting Started

Students who are interested in video or film can start by taking media courses in middle school or high school. Those courses may be "hands on." Some schools around the country have TV stations. Local and state laws have also reserved **public-access channels**. Those channels are for use by community members.

Other students can get training at local colleges and technical schools. In some cases, high school or college students can get **internships** at local TV stations. Internships are unpaid, short-term positions. They can provide people with their first professional experiences in their chosen field.

After high school or college, beginners often start as **production assistants**, or PAs. PA jobs may involve setting up cameras, lights, and other equipment. As PAs gain experience, they take on harder tasks.

Production assistants check cables and connections on the set of a talk show.

Shooting raw footage is only one part of making a film or video. People are also needed to write scripts, plan the shoot, and scout **locations**. After the video or film is shot, more people are needed to edit the footage and sell the finished product. Camera operators who work for small companies or are self-employed may do those tasks themselves.

Much video and film editing is now done with computers. A successful camera operator needs top-notch computer skills.

Same Jobs, Different Titles

Someone who works with a motion picture camera is called a **cinematographer** (sih-nuh-muh-TAH-gruh-fur). This term comes from *cinema*. That is another word for movies. A person who works with a video camera is called a **videographer** (vih-dee-AH-gruh-fur).

Could You Be a Camera Operator?

- Do you have a sharp eye and a steady hand?
- Do you enjoy creative projects?
- Do you like to take photos?
- Do you enjoy working with computers and high-tech gadgets?
- Would you like to visit new places and meet people?

If so, a career as a camera operator could bring your creative and tech skills into focus!

You can be a camera operator who travels for work or who works near home. You can work at a local TV station. You can make videos of local weddings, business meetings, and sports events. Whether close to home or far away, a career as a camera operator can take you where the action is!

CHAPTER 2
READY FOR ANYTHING

Goran Ehlme likes to shoot video in icy waters. He records seals and walruses in the Arctic. He also records whales and emperor penguins in Antarctica. Ehlme knows how to shoot video in

A career as a camera operator can take you to distant and exciting places. This film crew works in the Arctic.

harsh weather. Even he wasn't prepared for what happened on one of his recent trips to the Antarctic, however.

Ehlme told Animal Planet's *Up Close and Dangerous* that a large female seal attacked him during a shoot. At the time, he was traveling in a small boat. "Bang, she was up in my face, opening her jaws," he said. "I was totally terrified." Ehlme was knocked into the water. He scrambled back into the boat to safety.

Where the Action Is

Wherever there is something exciting to see, you'll likely find a video or film crew. News video crews often shoot footage of wars, hurricanes, fires, earthquakes, and volcanoes. Sports video crews cover everything from NBA games to the Olympics. Travel videos cover exciting vacation spots around the world.

Power Trip

To shoot great video, you need to do more than be in the right place at the right time. You need to get the correct shot. That means using the best equipment properly.

Along with your video camera and battery, you'll need backup gear. Depending on your camera's storage method, you'll need extra videocassettes or discs, memory cards, and batteries.

Backup batteries must be charged, but pros often carry battery chargers, too. They also carry long power cables to use when a standard electrical outlet is not within reach. Some pros carry a group of batteries worn around the waist. That way, they have several hours of power for long shoots.

Shaky Situations

Another tool camera operators rely on is a three-legged stand called a **tripod**. They attach the camera to the top of the stand. The height adjusts. The operator can raise or lower the camera. Tripods come in different sizes and can be folded to fit in tight spaces.

No one can hold a camera steady for very long. As time passes, the hand and arm get tired and start to shake. When that happens, the image becomes shaky, too. Sometimes a little "shake" is OK. For example, when showing a person running to shelter during a storm, the camera operator may want the image to look a little jumpy.

A tripod keeps a camera steady while shooting.

A camera operator uses a type of dolly to follow the action at the 2008 British Open golf tournament.

In most cases, though, camera operators want images that are steady. A tripod helps them achieve that goal.

On the Move

Often, a camera needs to move to follow the action. In a film or TV studio, the camera may be mounted on a **dolly**. A dolly is a rolling platform that can support the camera and its operator. It has a mechanical arm that can move the camera up and down.

Another way to get smooth video while moving a camera is with a **Steadicam**. A Steadicam operator wears a special vest. A mechanical arm extends from the vest. The arm supports a pole, or "sled," on which a video camera is mounted. The setup acts like a shock absorber. The Steadicam can produce a smooth shot even when the operator is moving quickly over uneven ground.

A Steadicam helps this camera operator shoot the plays at a football game.

On the Job: Videographer Alan Gleiner

Videographer Alan Gleiner works for WDBJ, a TV station in Roanoke, Virginia.

Q. Where did you get your training?

Gleiner: I took media courses in college. The last course I took was in educational television.

Q. How would you describe your job?

Gleiner: I'm not just a cameraman. I write. I direct. In some instances I also do sound and lighting. I edit. I choose music. All those things are required of a videographer.

Q. How have computers changed the way you work?

Gleiner: From the moment you step away from the shoot, you're dealing with computers. You need to know your way around computer hardware and software. You need to back up [make a copy of] everything!

Q. How has the video business changed?

Gleiner: People with a limited budget can buy video equipment. But you still need a good eye for telling the story.

Q. What do you enjoy most about being a videographer?

Gleiner: I enjoy it when a project comes together. I love it when scenes fit together well. It's like a jigsaw puzzle — visuals, action, music, and sound effects. I love it when all of those pieces come together successfully.

CHAPTER 3

SELLING IT

Video is powerful. It can spread information and change opinions. Video is also in demand. All the major TV networks pay for news and sports footage. TV programs use travel videos, as do hotel chains and cruise lines. Businesses and the armed forces hire camera operators to make training films. Museums show videos about works of art in their collections.

Some camera operators work for TV networks. Others form their own film or video production companies. These companies make money by selling the rights to use the films and videos they make. Buyers include TV stations, private businesses, and the government.

Pushing Products

Many film and video makers start their careers in advertising. Some shoot ads even after they become famous in other fields. Even though Spike Lee is among the most famous film directors in the United States, he still shoots ads for Nike.

Ads can be as short as fifteen seconds or as long as a minute or two. Some ads are simple. They may show

Camera operators sometimes shoot underwater to capture the perfect footage for travel videos.

What Is a Stock House?

Camera operators often send their films and videos to a **stock house**. A stock house keeps libraries of many different films and videos. Clips from those films and videos can often be viewed online. A company that wants to use a film or video pays a fee to the stock house. The stock house then shares this fee with the videographer or filmmaker. The greatest demand is for unusual or hard-to-get shots.

someone talking directly to the camera. These ads can be very inexpensive to make.

Other ads may cost millions or more. Some feature top stars. Some include popular music and eye-popping special effects. Many ads use humor as a selling tool.

Different Types of Ads

One kind of ad is a **movie trailer**. When shown in a movie theater, a trailer may run two minutes or more. When edited for TV, a trailer is much shorter. People can also download movie trailers from the Internet.

Soccer star David Beckham (far left) takes a break while a camera operator moves the camera during a soft drink commercial.

Money in the Bank

Students who enjoy working with video can make a difference. Students at Mount Si High School in Snoqualmie, Washington, made a video for their local food bank. First, students met with community leaders. They learned about the neighborhood's Helping Hand food program. Next, students worked together to write a script. Finally, they shot and edited a video. The video was broadcast in local movie theaters and on TV. It informed people about the food bank's growing financial needs. The students' video helped raise $30,000 for the food program.

In election years, political ads fill the TV screen. Those ads may be positive or negative. For positive ads, video crews get flattering shots of the person running for office. Negative ads are shot or edited to show opponents in a very unflattering way.

Some TV ads last up to thirty minutes. Those are called **infomercials**. They often have an on-screen host. The host may show how a product works. He or she may interview people who talk about the item. Infomercials advertise all kinds of things, from hair-care products to vacation homes.

CHAPTER 4

GLAMOUR JOBS, BASIC SKILLS

Imagine that you are standing on a film set halfway around the world. You're shooting a huge action movie. The lighting is perfect. Your camera captures the magic that will be seen on the big screen.

Now imagine you're on the set of a music video. The rhymes are fresh. The dance moves are dazzling. The song is a monster hit. Your shooting and special effects make the visuals jump off the screen.

Mastering the Basics

Do those sound like dream jobs to you? Many camera operators share the same dream. The competition is tough. If you want the best jobs in video or film, you'll need skill and the desire to work hard.

You will probably start out as a production assistant. First, you must master the basics. You must learn how to use different cameras and other equipment. You must learn how to set up lighting for a shot. Then you can start taking creative control of your own productions.

Camera operators at MTV Studios often shoot celebrities, such as pop musician Pink.

Light and Dark

Professional camera operators know their cameras the way musicians know their instruments. Modern film and video cameras have many automatic features. Those features make filming or taping easy for casual users who just want to point and shoot. Pros want as much control over the shoot as possible, however. They want to choose specific settings that will produce exactly the look they want.

For example, pros control **exposure**, or the amount of light in the shot. A camera operator controls exposure by adjusting the **iris**. Like the iris in the human eye, this part of the camera determines how much light passes through the lens. On a sunny day, the light is very bright. The camera operator may need to close the camera's iris a bit to let in less light. The situation is different on a stormy evening. The light may be too dim. The camera operator may open the iris to let in more light.

On the Job: Spike Jonze

Spike Jonze has had many dream jobs. First he was a BMX biker and a skateboarder. Then he was a dancer, stunt performer, and videographer. He has shot award-winning videos with the Beastie Boys, Weezer, Fatboy Slim, and Ludacris. He has made ads for top companies. He even directed some of the wildest films of the last decade. His most recent film is *Where the Wild Things Are*, due out in 2009.

The controls for exposure and focus can be changed on professional video and film cameras.

Staying Focused

When a person shoots a scene, some parts of the image may look sharp. Other parts may look blurry. The part of the shot that is clear is in **focus**. A properly focused shot guides the eye to the most important part of a scene. At a basketball game, for example, the camera usually stays focused on the player with the ball. The moving image guides the viewer's eye toward the shooter and away from fans and sideline players.

Valley Community Library
739 River Street

Focus may change depending on the subject. In a show about bees, insects in a hive might be shown in very sharp focus. In a romantic travel video, softer edges look more inviting. Camera operators want cameras that give them as much control over focus as possible.

Planning for Success

To make great films or videos, you need to know how to plan a shoot. The following sample plan covers three stages.

The first stage is **preproduction**, or the period before shooting begins.

During preproduction, you:

- Research subject and write script
- Make budget and shooting schedule
- Choose locations for shooting
- Hire actors and crew
- Buy or rent special equipment

The second stage is the **production**. That is the period when the shoot takes place.

During production, you:

- Secure the set
- Set up the lights and cameras
- Direct the actors or talent

An editor adds music and other sound effects to a video during postproduction.

- Control the amount of shooting time
- Reshoot if needed

The **postproduction** stage is the period after the shoot.

During postproduction, you:
- Add music and sound effects
- Edit raw video or film footage on computer
- Create final high-quality version

You may do some of those tasks yourself. You may hire other people to do some of the tasks for you. If you are making a low-budget film or video, you may need to ask friends and family members to help. For a big-budget production, you would hire experienced pros.

CHAPTER 5

GOING DIGITAL

Videos are created, edited, and stored on computers. Computer software also lets video makers add music, special effects, and titles. Today, you can't be a video pro without being computer-savvy, too.

From Every Angle

If you want to see the future of video and computers, look at sports programs. During a NASCAR race, cameras aren't just placed around the track. Each race car may carry as many as three cameras.

Editors review footage from many different cameras in the control room.

One camera sits in the driving compartment. It can swivel to point in any direction. A second camera looks out over the rear bumper. A third may be mounted on the top of the car. The camera operator uses a computer to work these cameras by remote control. Small cameras are also mounted near the driver's feet. Another tiny camera is mounted inside the driver's helmet. That camera looks out through the driver's face shield. That way, viewers can see the race exactly as the driver sees it.

Summer Programs

Young people can get hands-on video experience in summer camps. The New York Film Academy in New York City runs summer camps in film and acting for 10- to 13-year-olds. The academy also has programs for older students. The iD Film Academy in San Francisco, California, also runs a summer session for teens.

The School of Cinema and Performing Arts, or SOCAPA, offers summer filmmaking programs for teens, too. SOCAPA courses take place in New York City; Los Angeles, California; and Burlington, Vermont.

Camera operators face physical challenges at sports events, such as this football game. The camera operator gets inside the huddle by lifting the camera.

Slow-Mo and High-Tech

TV networks are inventive when covering football. They place super slow-motion cameras on the sidelines. Those cameras enable replays that show every detail in super-sharp, high-def video. Remote-control cameras move back and forth on wires high above the field.

In the coming years, computers will advance. Video and film cameras will also improve. Those changes will affect camera operators at every level. To keep pace with changes in technology, students should learn as much as possible about computer hardware and software. Staying on the cutting edge of new technology is just one way of getting a great shot!

CAMERA OPERATOR

OUTLOOK

- About 27,000 Americans have jobs as video or film camera operators. Another 21,000 work as video or film editors.

- The number of jobs in the video and film industry is expected to grow about 12 percent between 2006 and 2016. Competition is tough.

WHAT YOU'LL DO

- Many camera operators work in TV and motion picture studios. Others travel around the world to shoot news events, sports contests, interviews, travel videos, and other footage.

- Some camera operators make training films for business and the armed forces. Some pros get paid to make videos of important life events, such as weddings.

- Much of your work will be done with a camera in your hands. You may also need to write scripts, hire actors, choose locations, and edit footage.

WHAT YOU'LL NEED

- You will need to take video courses in high school or college. You will also train on the job.

- A camera operator needs a spirit of adventure to shoot in difficult or dangerous locations.

- If you work on your own, you'll need to buy a professional camera and editing equipment.

- Excellent computer skills are essential.

WHAT YOU'LL EARN

- Camera operators earn about $40,000 a year. Experienced professionals may earn a yearly salary of $80,000 or more.

Source: U.S. Department of Labor, Bureau of Labor Statistics

GLOSSARY

cinematographer — a person who operates a film camera

documentary — a film or video that gives an in-depth view of a single topic, often one with social or political significance

dolly — a rolling platform that supports a camera and its operator

exposure — the amount of light in a shot

focus — the camera control that sets which parts of a scene look blurry or sharp

infomercials — television ads that may last as long as 30 minutes and that look like typical TV shows

internships — short-term "starter" jobs that are often held by young people with little to no experience

iris — the part of a video camera that determines how much light passes through the lens

locations — places where a video is shot

movie trailer — a preview or an ad for a film

postproduction — the period after shooting, when a film or video is put into final form

preproduction — the period before shooting begins

production — the period during which a video or film is shot

production assistants (PAs) — workers who set up lights, cameras, and other equipment at a shoot

public-access channels — channels that are used by nonprofit groups such as schools and community groups

raw footage — unedited film or video straight from the camera

Steadicam — a device that produces a smooth shot even when the camera operator is moving quickly over uneven ground

stock house — a business that keeps libraries of films or videos that other companies pay to use

tripod — a three-legged stand that supports a camera

videographer — a person who works with a video camera

TO FIND OUT MORE

Books

Attack of the Killer Video Book: Tips and Tricks for Young Directors. Mark Shulman and Hazlitt Krog (Annick Press, 2004)

Backstage at a Music Video. High Interest Books: Backstage Pass (series). Holly Cefrey (Children's Press, 2003)

Girl Director: A How-To Guide for the First-Time Flat-Broke Film and Video Maker. Andrea Richards (Ten Speed Press, 2005)

So You Want to Be a Film or TV Director? Careers in Film and Television (series). Amy Dunkleberger (Enslow Publishers, 2007)

So You Want to Be a Film or TV Editor? Careers in Film and Television (series). Amy Dunkleberger (Enslow Publishers, 2007)

Web Sites

National Geographic: Videos
video.nationalgeographic.com/video
Explore a rich collection of videos from around the world.

Video Camera Tutorials
www.mediacollege.com/video/camera
Check out this guide to shot types, camera angles, and other video camera basics.

Welcome to the Video Guide
pblmm.k12.ca.us/TechHelp/VideoHelp/VideoGuide.html
A school system in California offers detailed advice on how to plan, shoot, and edit a video project.

INDEX

About the Author

Geoffrey M. Horn has written more than three dozen books for young people and adults, along with hundreds of articles for encyclopedias and other works. He lives in southwestern Virginia, in the foothills of the Blue Ridge Mountains, with his wife, their collie, and six cats. He dedicates this book to Sarah, Alan, and Jonas.